A Mendocino Portfolio

poetry Cynthia Frank
photography Hannes Krebs

Q.E.D. Press Fort Bragg, California 1988

Book design: Mark Gatter & Chuck Hathaway
Typography: Comp-Type, Inc.
Layout: Mark Gatter, Brina Leopold

Library of Congress Number 88-061393
ISBN 0-936609-12-5

For more information, please write:

Q.E.D. Press
155 Cypress Street
Fort Bragg, CA 95437

Dedicated to the Mendocino Coast,
its future and its people.
They gave us the inspiration
to create this book.

Acknowledgements

We are truly grateful to Cordelia Shampanier for her continued support throughout the years it took to bring this work together. She graciously provided us with gallery space at Fiddles and Cameras and believed enough in the quality of our work to help make this book possible.

We would like to give credit to Steve Ryan for his exceptional film-developing service and his personal attention to our sometimes demanding deadlines; to Dave Bellew, Sally Peck and Ben Obitz for their darkroom expertise; to John Fremont for his expert typography, common sense and patience; to Leonard Cirino and Pat McKay for their painstaking proofreading and comments; to John Berryman for his *Dream Songs*; to Karin Faulkner for her late-night editorial and consultation services above and beyond the call; to Chuck Hathaway and Camille Ranker of Mendocino Graphics for always being available with their expertise and encouragement; to Bob Avery, who knew we would publish this book eventually; to Charlie Sleight for his friendship and supporting wisdom; to Hilda Pertha for her refined insight into the essence of our work; to Janice Van Horn of the Copy Shop for her flying fingers and tireless good humor; and to Tyler Lincoln and the members of the Symphony of the Redwoods for their unruffled composure during rehearsal of the Brahms Second Concerto.

We would also like to thank Olaf Palm and the Mendocino Woodlands Art Camp, the Mendocino Music Festival, Lolli Jacobsen and the Mendocino Weavers Guild, *Arts and Entertainment* Magazine, the Mendocino Art Center, *North Coast News* and other local media, Antonia Lamb, Shady Grove, James Krenov, Larry Fuente and the Fourth of July paraders, Jean-Paul, Bonnie Blum, Mose Allison, the old Seagull, Daniel Webster, W.C. Fields, the Mendocino fog and all the people whose pictures appear on these pages.

We are singularly indebted to the seal who made a special appearance in the photograph accompanying *During the Invasion of a Distant Island.*

And, finally, we're very thankful to that spirit of camaraderie which prevailed throughout the ten years we worked on this book.

Cynthia Frank
Hannes Krebs

September, 1988

I'd rather be here

Casting Beyond the Moon

(for Ocean Sanctuary)

The sea extends
The pull of gravity

Engraves her mood
Upon the heavens

Multiplies
Astronomically induced thoughts

The ocean sings
Startled birds change their course

Sea and stars reach
Out . . . their sparkling hands

Anchor us
Along these jeweled wings of earth

bloodties
sea palm bristles
across kelp-corded wrists
to the knuckled-
under at the last
rocks
the salt flood hisses
bloodties

And the Ocean Called Me Down the Rocks, Saying

Always
I am the same
Unruled
Unsaked

Full of eyes and teeth
Deep breasted
Great
Furrowed cheeks running
Rivers
Into this surging
Mouth

My salt tongue will deliver you
Or lash you to the rail

(Press your fingers
To the corners of your eyes
At the bridge of your nose
Mark the depth to your brain)

You flatter me with your lust
I could shatter you with a whim

1

Her fear is a coracle in wartime.
She quietly, obliquely approaches an island.
Her smoke smudge appears often and without warning
along the horizon.
She is wary of submarines and arrives unexpectedly
to avoid detection.
She carries depth charges of pride
to this low island of her dreams
where the enemy is housebound
watching the sea, and also afraid
of submarines.

She seeks shelter in the rocky coastline.
Nosing in, tentative,
bobbing in the cold, green sea.

She knows her home port,
her landfalls and destinations.
Only the long seascape of the journey
with its deep folds of green water, is
unpredictable.

Distances have always fooled her.

2

Her anger is a dusky bittern
that feeds upon doubt.
She stalks, up to her slim ankles
in the foam at rivermouth.
She turns her imperative head
and impales the dumb fish
one by one.

As her anger flies
she sights watchfully
the diligent patterns
of alien shadows beneath the waves,
casting their long net for a small boat,
and counts them among the fishes for her dinner.
Aloft, her feet are two small question marks
against the slate blue belly of the sky.

Her anger knows no regret
nor mercy.
Neither does she sing.

3

Her violence is an aborigine
who knows the island
is held to the sea floor
by a single strand of ancestral hair.

The sea carries her
so close to the rocks,
the lips, the lost faces
that cry, "Doubt,
you carrion of faith!"

This aborigine apprehends her life
as she paces the shore
eyes narrow and trained
on the seam where the sun
falls into the basket of the sea.

We will find the native
strung up over her craft like a harp.
The sails of a lesser ship
between the blades of her shoulders
driving her forward.

During the Invasion of a Distant Island

Surf smelt
Leap in the net.
A sea lion glides in,
Moustaches dragging—we trust that
We are

Safe here.
Sunlight calls out
From behind her cloud-loom
With kelp-brown, driftwood, bottle-green,
Weft . . . warp.

Apple
Twigs over coals
Just up the beach. Coffee,
Biscuits. Crunchy fingerlings, bones
And all.

Ready
For the next throw?
The slap of saltwater
Against a furred cheek the only
Answer.

October 25, 1983

MacKerricher Beach

I stride along
No longer looking
For sand rubies or seaweed bulbs
Only the salt rush against my legs

Walking on
Buoyant sand
In waves my toes
Drift deep
Into the place
Where the continent
Crouches down to meet the water

Flung out to reach
The Northwest Passage
The Sea of Japan
Kamchatka stretching
Toward the moon

I look inland a moment
Away across the sand
My mother

Not even pipers announce her presence
She doesn't move with grace
Or sit in comfort
By the sea
Her riverine wit
Her black jade style
Yearn for earth
For muddy deltas

She is the bitter root
More than washed, barrened by storms
No longer the strong feet
The holding to the sky

Soaking in the hard cold edge
Of winter sun
Too hungry to be given up for lost

Driftwood
On a bank of shifting clay

For Those Who Try to Hold the Picture Still

(and those who came too late)

And if the ocean
with her salty divination
insists upon what we cannot see,

there are still a few
who believe that truth
wins out

Though what you see first
some mornings:
the ocean blooming with white
flowers in the offshore wind
is the only thing that is
not for sale,

if you watch us closely enough
you can figure out how
we do it

(The romance is only
what we pretend
to love as we devour
our own tales)

We see through
ourselves
to the redwoods
and the waves

Paintings end in wooden corners
paper embraces these words
but the dancer's body
and the fine frame
of the sculptor's hands
show us why
we begin again

here

Cabinetmaker

simply
a caress

yet
the plane

bites
amber curls

sawdust
settles in

light
and air

layers
of history

once
fastened tightly

now
spring free

Queen of Cups

Her naked skin
is the conductor.

In the light and shadow
of this solution,
the nature of the artist
is change.

The concertina player's tunes paint an afternoon
already fragrant with linseed oil

The painter, playing
on the fine redolence of intuition
exposes the angular melody of a tilted jawline

as power moves through mastery
and control
to abandon

and harmonize
with chance

On Carving an Eagle

(for Byrd Baker)

Fly!
That's what I want to do.
This old Byrd's gonna learn to fly!

An illusion. *Damn*—
Yes! It gets bigger
When you walk away
And bigger
When you're up close

Like looking at your own cupped hand
Then stretching out the fingers.
It's all in the wings!

Clear overtones climb the Prussian blue trail
of the Brahms Second Concerto

The conductor, soundpost of this resonating body
Ignites each small silence with his baton

The flames, reflected
on the broad brow of the first cellist

Are passed down the strings and woodwinds
In chestnut, ebony and silver flashes

Under the recording engineer's discerning gaze,
the needles dance

He cups the oracle to his ear
like a sea shell

Surface Tension

if music is a liquid
or, say, the skin of a timpano

and the audience is the air
say, or a solo violin

then is a symphony

        (due to molecular forces)
that quiet breath between movements

rehearsal breaks
the patient counting of measures by the percussionist

(which exists in the surface film)
in the bassoon player, the original score,
in the conductor, the listener, the lover

(of all liquids)
of all music
(and tends to bring the contained volume)

the listener forward in her seat
        (into a form
        having the least superficial area?)

And what of
        particles lying below the film
those silent tears out in the darkened auditorium
those separate lives
striving for what they believe
they believe

(being equally acted on from all sides)
the composer and the composed
the music and the musicians
the coffee and the champagne of intermission
the news of a friend's death
that message finally come from across the worlds?

Are they
(in equilibrium
as to forces of cohesion)
and the audience and the music
are they
stuck to each other like dark, wild honey?

(and those in the film)
those not touched
and those touched beyond fear
beyond imagination or daring
are they
(on the whole attracted inward?)

(tension results)
tears
applause
breath
(we measure the work done in bringing)
the couple in the third row
the unforgiven son
the woman with the crying child, lonely
outcasts
(molecules

from the interior
to the surface)
of this song

Ensemble

Sax, horn, bone and bass/drum
solos

Band and dancer/striking
poses

Their hands/rhododendron
branches

Finger-cymbals or leaf-arrows
turning in the storm

To a barefoot woman
arched over the grass

Seventh Son

He's makin' everything easy
Right on time
The black piano
Dances in the sun
With his white shirt
And old straw hat

We run our fingers through the grass
He answers back on the white keys
We dance and lounge, tap and tan

He sings us a song, no explanations
We nod to his dream's direct connection
And push on down to the earth below

Yes, he says
Lean with me over the black keys
Into this blue afternoon

We nod our assent to the sun
He's makin' everything easy
Right on time

Salmon Barbecue

Family secret and garlic
Thank you, salmon

Wrapped in fresh dill
Thank you

Lemon pips flying
Thank you, salmon

Steamed in brown paper
Thank you

Charcoal and butter
Thank you, salmon

On big-bellied t-shirts
Thank you

The men cook for us, here
Thank you, salmon

With old fashioned curve-fingered spatulas
Thank you

Horseradish running down our chins
Thank you, salmon

Seen through the smoke
Thank you

Old friends, old jokes
Thank you, salmon
Thank you

Big River

In this salt and pewter morning
the body of the land prepares itself
for burial at sea.

Tight fistfuls of sand fall
at the child's feet. My own
hands hold the grains
against the grain. Fog quickens. Together
we push the limits of this silver negative.

As Big River meets the sea,
sienna and dusty jade divide
the bodies of the beloved waters.
We struggle against it all; deny the tide.

El Niño

Doubt digs wells. (Or is it memory?)
We rotate the holes, shower at a friend's house,
Munch our tight dusty blackberries.
No public restrooms. No water,
We're out of business.
One driller says
Punch through the rock
There's enough for everyone
Who's got the money
(Who *gets* the money?)
The best restaurant in town
Got a $6,000 dry hole.
They punched through,
But it wasn't worth the trip.
Try to avoid the neighbors
(in aerobics class)
Up the hill.
(or at the post office)
You've struck clear,
(walking the Headlands)
No sand,
(in line at Mendosa's)
Just across the property line,
(at the bank)
They've run dry.

First Cumulus Over Kelley House

Rain fingers our dust-bitten hopes
Sudden fins twist in the derelict pond

Kerosene Moon

(for Grandpa Josh)

Across the center of the waters
One small breeze
Ten pale moons
Rise from the fingers
Of this unborn child

We Take It With Us

we take it with us
this stance by the smoking fire
we learned from no grandfather

we take it with us
the grain of the wood
the snap of grasshoppers in the clearing

we take it with us
the handmade house
bound on the back of our truck

we take it with us
the broken horizon
that is our California

we take it with us
to a ring of bare earth
surrounded by trees

we take it with us
without calling in experts or digital watches
we know when the tide changes

we take it with us
the white half moons of our fingers
tell us we are still holding on

Near Hendy Woods

The impotent speak of her scars

saying, note the clan membership,
the initiation into secret practices.

Pimps hawk her green virtues
in the city streets.

The grove's last rings
unfurl among serpents.

If the mycelial net unravels
not even the ground will break her fall.

Parley

A shadow kites across the photograph.
Black and white, laid on the table. Hanging

On the wall, the photograph postulates
Quality of Light. The poem, Adjective.

Poetry connects spirit with mind.
That leads life apart from matter.

And so, the body is omitted
And dancer separated from the dance;

Photographs might portray
Outer reality, frozen in time. Yet

As light travels, image and observer
Veer in concert.

The photographer's hand
Dodges across an artificial night

The dancer turns,
I edit, and rewrite.

St. People

Street people are more intimate with the police
Street people are adept at interior decorating
Street people are thought to have first names only

Our children know street people
Have a different reason
For being on the beach at dawn

Street people are given drugs
For free street people can be dangerous
Everyone's got the notion they know when

Street people turn to no one but themselves
In the rain, old plastic bags and tape—
Even newspapers take on new meaning

Sometimes street people are committed
They pay a special tax to the Man who knows
Where they all sleep

To the Man who says
Who you with honey
Come on outta there

Street people rummage in dumpsters
Wear their tattoos into high class stores
Have dirty fingernails for no good reason

Street people carry on conversatons with the wind
They might ask the congregation to pray for them
(This is a different risk than the holy are used to)

Street people disappear sometimes
And sometimes street people come
Back to Main Street

And stand on the Headlands
Street people come back like neighbors
Come back after vacation with their carry-on luggage

Carry on street people

Alphonso's

Musicians, just passing through town
always stop at Alphonso's

Look what I found, they cry
I can't believe what he has in there
I'll bet there's not another recording of this
(Wagner, Kirkby, Caballe, Copland)
on the whole West Coast, and

incense (like Vermont before the mud begins)
cigar boxes, corncob pipes, Hormel's chili,
penknives, string, jerky
for our walk on the beach

The cat curls more tightly in the window
between the sun-faded sign
offering him for sale
and the letter
from the cat
pleading
for more appropriate dinner music

Cutting A Figure

Eleven years in Mendocino

His collected conversation could be
mustered in a fleeting, gap-toothed grin

To the greenhorn and the wary
his desires are tangled
as his dreads

But the children call him Owl

Conjunction:
Mendocino/Mexico City, 1985

late afternoon in September
the skin of fog and apple light
tightens high above the tattered
pygmy cedar and empire-waisted pine

a hummingbird thrums suddenly
past, and

how we carry ourselves
falters, as

a jet contrail portions out the sky, the

epicenter of what we have denied
closes in

September 19 & 21, 1985

RICAN
SKEY
-CA.-55
80 PROO
9 LITER

And then there's . . .

the Fourth of July

The Fourth of July

So—you thought you knew
About home town celebrations?
Thought the chicken pluckers
Were the livin' end?

Try this party
Straight past
The pages of National Geographic

Give us a hand
Or a duck
A petrified uncle
Some leopard skin
With our sister inside

Welcome to the cliffside mind
What makes us tick
Is what we throw away
What we break
Or forget
That extra hand
We can use it
The lost swans
And the children, too

Parade

Some, misunderstanding the intrinsic love,
might accuse Larry Fuente,
the solar-powered rock band
or the "Bread Not Bombs" bakery
of subversive activities

But not the man in the stet-foam hat,
the breakdancers, or the child
on stilts toppling his way up Lansing Street

From "Auntie Sam Sez I Want You To Stay Home"
to "Peace is Patriotic"
we've never learned to march in step

And it's no fault

I'd rather be here
than in Philadelphia

Wildlife Gallery
OF MENDOCINO

HOHNER

PEOPLE
for a
NUCLEAR
FREE
FUTURE

Notes

Most of the photographs in this book were taken with a Hasselblad 500-CM using 80mm Zeiss Planar f2.8/80mm and Zeiss Sonnar f4/150mm lenses. Other photographs were taken with a Nikon FM using Mikro-Nikkor f2.8/55mm, Series E 36-72mm, and Series E 75-150mm lenses. Films used were principally Ilford XP-1 developed in XP-1 Developer, and Kodak Tri-X 400 ISO. All photographs were developed and printed on the Mendocino Coast. *Winter Evening in Mendocino* was shot with a Rolleiflex 3.5f using a Zeiss Planar f3.5/75mm lens.

The Photographs

About the Authors

Born in Bavaria, Germany, raised and educated in Chile and Argentina, Hannes Krebs moved to the United States in 1961. After many adventures (the subject of his next book), national and international photo awards and exhibits, Hannes settled on the Mendocino Coast and soon became intimately acquainted with the people and the spirit of the Mendocino Coast.

"There is so much to photograph and write about here. Smells, sounds, the people and their creativity, textures, the ever-changing light, the mist and fog and, always, the moods of the ocean."

Cynthia Frank is a second-generation Californian. She teaches poetry workshops through California Poets in the Schools, is co-founder of **Rain Straight Down**, and sings with **Alchemy**, an a cappella trio which has been performing in Mendocino County for more than 12 years. She is a publisher and president of Comp-Type, Inc.

"I want to convey the particular temperament of the North Coast—where our struggles with solitude and loneliness, rural and urban lifestyles, environment and industry, community and isolation are so vital. People get healed here."

This book grew out of a restaurant conversation between Hannes and Cynthia in 1978. It has been a labor of love.

Colophon

This book was typeset in 14 and 16 point Zapf Chancery on a Comp-Edit typesetter and printed on 100 lb. enamel paper.